OLYSLAGER AUTO LIBRARY

British Cars of the Early Forties 1940-1946

compiled by the OLYSLAGER ORGANISATION
edited by Bart H. Vanderveen

FREDERICK WARNE & Co Ltd
London and New York

THE OLYSLAGER AUTO LIBRARY

This book is one of a growing range of titles on major transport subjects. Titles published so far include:

The Jeep
Half-Tracks
Scammell Vehicles
Fire-Fighting Vehicles
Earth-Moving Vehicles
Wreckers and Recovery Vehicles
Passenger Vehicles 1893–1940
Buses and Coaches from 1940
Fairground and Circus Transport

American Cars of the 1930s
American Cars of the 1940s
American Cars of the 1950s

British Cars of the Early Thirties
British Cars of the Late Thirties
British Cars of the Early Forties
British Cars of the Late Forties

Copyright © Olyslager Organisation BV 1974

Library of Congress Catalog Card No. 73-89827

ISBN 0 7232 1755 6

Filmset and printed in Great Britain
by BAS Printers Limited, Wallop, Hampshire

576.873

INTRODUCTION

Third in the Olyslager Auto Library series of pictorial histories of British cars, this volume deals with a most eventful era, namely the years 1940 and 1945/46, and the period of all-out war production in between.

In 1940 civilian car production decreased gradually to virtually nil, giving way to the manufacturing of a wide variety of war equipment. In addition to military staff cars, light trucks and armoured cars the British car industry turned out a tremendous variety of other materials, varying from ammunition boxes to complete aeroplanes. The war was hardly over before many manufacturers resumed civilian production, most of them in the summer and autumn of 1945. These cars, the majority of which differed very little from those of 1939/40, are dealt with as 1946 models. With a few exceptions, such as the brand-new Jowett and 1½-Litre Riley, these 1940/1946 models were superseded about 1948 by the first real post-war designs, which are comprehensively covered in the companion volume, *British Cars of the Late Forties*.

In 1946 the British Motor Industry celebrated their fiftieth anniversary. Initiated by the Society of Motor Manufacturers and Traders, these national celebrations took the form of exhibitions and impressive Grand Cavalcades in many major cities. The Midland Cavalcade (Coventry and Birmingham), for example, held on 21 September, consisted of a procession of no fewer than 320 vehicles dating from 1896 and including examples of all the latest production models, most of which are shown in this book.

Piet Olyslager MSIA, MSAE, KIVI

1940

1940 The year 1940 was the first full year of war, and civilian car production dwindled to just under 2000 units. By November, the total number of cars on British roads was 1,348,817, almost 280,000 fewer than a year before. The number of hackneys in use, however, had increased by over 14,000 to 81,484. Many cars were commandeered by the Army and others were converted into ambulances, canteen vans, etc. Some manufacturers supplied military versions of their civilian cars direct to the War Office, the Admiralty and other government authorities. Some of these are included in the following pages and there are more in the 1941–45 section. Armoured vehicle production was already in full swing. 947 AFVs (armoured fighting vehicles) were produced in 1939, followed by 7441 in 1940, increasing steadily to 31,851 in 1943. In 1939, fewer than half a million people were employed in the production and repair of motor vehicles in the UK. In the peak year, 1943, this number had risen to 1,121,800, about half of whom were part-time female workers. Many garages throughout the country were engaged in the overhaul of military vehicles, as well as in the assembly of Lend-Lease vehicles which arrived in CKD (completely knocked down) packs from North America. Others, sometimes in their showrooms, actually produced components for the big manufacturers under sub-contracts.

4B Aston Martin Atom

4A Alvis 4·3-Litre

4A: **Alvis** 4·3-Litre with four-door Tourer bodywork by Cross & Ellis. Unlike the Tourer, the 1940 Alvis Saloon and Drophead Coupé did not have running boards; the wings on these models faired into the sides of the scuttle. The six-cylinder engine had a cubic capacity of 4387 cc (92 × 110 mm) and was rated at 31·48 HP. Other Alvis offerings in 1940 were the 12/70 (1842-cc Four), Silver Crest (2362- and 2762-cc Six) and Speed 25 (3571-cc Six).

4B: **Aston Martin** Atom Saloon, work on which had started in 1939. The car was completed during the war and was the first Aston Martin to have the tubular space frame chassis designed by Claude Hill. By the end of the war it had Hill's new 2-litre OHC engine. This 'one-off' was the direct ancestor of all post-war Aston Martins, production of which started in 1948 (DB1).

1940

5A Austin Eight

5B Austin Twelve

5C Ford Anglia

5A: **Austin** 8 HP Two-seater, Model AP, was a modification of the civilian type tourer, produced for the British Army for liaison and similar duties. It had two seats and a folding windscreen. The slightly slanted louvres in the bonnet side panels were a distinguishing feature. In the background are Austin-built four-stretcher military ambulances (Model K2Y).

5B: **Austin** 12 HP Saloon, Model HRB, as produced from August 1939. It was completely redesigned as compared with the preceding Model HRA Light Twelve of 1938/39. The wheelbase was 8 ft 10¼ in, but this was shortened to 8 ft 8½ in in 1945 (Model HS1). Production ceased in 1947. The 12 HP had a 1535-cc side-valve Four engine.

5C: **Ford** Anglia 8 HP, Model E04A, was introduced in 1939 and continued after the war with minor changes, until 1948. It was a face-lifted improved development of the 1937–39 Eight Model 7Y. It had a 933-cc (56·6 × 92·5 mm) four-cylinder engine, 7 ft 6 in wheelbase and two-door bodywork. Its companion, the 10 HP Prefect Model E93A, had 63·5-mm bore (1172 cc), 7 ft 10 in wheelbase and four-door bodywork.

1940

page 6

6A Hillman Minx

6C Hillman Fourteen

6B Hillman Minx

6A: **Hillman** Minx in its 1939/40 form. The engine was the proven 9·8 HP 1185-cc side-valve Four and the radiator grille was integral with the rear-hinged bonnet. The car shown features wartime headlamp masks and white-painted bumpers. During the war it was produced mainly in Light Utility form for the Services (see page 22).
6B: **Hillman** Minx in typical wartime London setting. 1940 Minx prices were from £165 to £210.
6C: **Hillman** Fourteen was the only other type produced by the Hillman Motor Car Co. in 1939/40. The body styling resembled that of the Minx, but the car was almost 2 ft longer and had a 13·96 HP 1944-cc side-valve Four engine. Prices ranged from £238 to £285. Unlike the Minx, the Fourteen was not reintroduced after the war. Compared with 1938/39 models, the 1940 Fourteen had revised bonnet side strips, Lockheed instead of Bendix brakes and Luvax piston-type shock absorbers. Most vehicles were supplied to the Army and the Royal Air Force.

1940

7A Humber Super Snipe

7C Humber Pullman

7B Humber Super Snipe

7D Humber Pullman

7A: **Humber** Super Snipe was a carry-over from 1939. The body styling had much in common with the Hillman Fourteen (*q.v.*), but featured a built-out luggage boot and a distinctive radiator grille. The engine was a 26·9 HP 4086-cc side-valve Six. The Humber Sixteen and Snipe looked similar but had smaller-bore engines of 2576- and 3181-cc capacity respectively. All had 9 ft 6 in wheelbase.

7B: **Humber** Super Snipe in austere military livery. In the Services this model was officially known as the Snipe, although it had the 4086-cc engine. On these cars the rear end was modified for improved 'angle of departure'. Tyres were India 7.00-16 'Aero Cushion', but the later production had 9.00-13 military type (see page 23).

7C: **Humber** Pullman Limousine in RAF livery. The Army and Navy used similar cars. The Pullman had the same 4086-cc engine as the Super Snipe, but a wheelbase of 10 ft $7\frac{1}{2}$ in.

7D: **Humber** Pullman Limousine in British Army khaki livery. Some were supplied with formal black paint finish for domestic use. Most Pullmans for the Services were fitted with the roof luggage rail, as shown.

1940

8A: Lagonda Motors Ltd of Staines offered several high-quality chassis with varying wheelbase lengths and either 29·13 HP 4467-cc six-cylinder or 41·8 HP 4480-cc V-12-cylinder engine (Models LG6 and V12 respectively). An attractive Drophead Coupé is shown in this wartime advertisement.

8B: Lea-Francis, in 1940, offered two basic models which were substantially the same except for engine size (11·9 HP 69 × 100 mm and 12·8 HP 72 × 100 mm, both four-cylinders). Both four- and six-light (shown) saloons were offered. In 1945 the bore of the larger engine was increased to 75 mm.

8C: Morris Ten (or Ten-Four), Series M, was continued from 1939 and was reintroduced in 1945 in substantially the same form. It was a four-door Saloon with 9·99 HP 1140-cc four-cylinder engine and 7 ft 10 in wheelbase. Its smaller sister was the Eight, Series E, with 8·05 HP 918-cc engine.

8A Lagonda V12

8B Lea-Francis 12·8 HP

8C Morris Ten

1940

9A: Riley Twelve of 1939/40 was one of two models offered, the other being the 16 HP Big Four. The Twelve, or 1½-Litre, had a 1496-cc (69 × 100 mm) four-cylinder engine of 11·9 HP rating. Prices were from £310 to £335.

9B: Rover Ten was available as Saloon and Coupé (shown). The 1389-cc (66·5 × 100 mm) four-cylinder engine was of 10·8 HP rating. Wheelbase was 8 ft 9½ in, tyre size 4.75-17.

9C: Rover Twelve Saloon with 1496-cc (69 × 100 mm) four-cylinder 11·8 HP engine. Wheelbase was 9 ft 4 in, tyre size 5.25-17. Also available as four-light Sports Saloon.

9D: Rover Fourteen Sports Saloon had 14·9 HP six-cylinder engine of 1901-cc cubic capacity (63·5 × 100 mm). Tyre size and wheelbase were 5.50-17 and 9 ft 7 in respectively for all 1939/40 Rover six-cylinder models. The Rover Sixteen was similar in appearance but had ventilating doors in the bonnet sides, like the Twenty (q.v.).

9A Riley Twelve

9C Rover Twelve

9B Rover Ten

9D Rover Fourteen

10A Rover Twenty

10B Singer Super Ten

10C SS Jaguar 2½-Litre

10A: **Rover** Twenty Drophead Coupé. This body style was available also on the Fourteen and Sixteen chassis. The Twenty had a 19·8 HP 2512-cc (73 × 100 mm) six-cylinder engine and in Saloon form cost £425. The cheapest Rover was the Ten at £275.

10B: **Singer** Super Ten Saloon cost £203 10s. Also offered were the 8·93 HP Bantam and 11·47 HP Twelve. The Super Ten had a 9·8 HP 1185-cc (63 × 95 mm) engine and 7 ft 11 in wheelbase. All models had four cylinders. Super Ten and Twelve Saloons were reintroduced after the war, supplemented by a Nine Roadster.

10C: **SS** Jaguar 2½-Litre Drophead Coupé cost £435 and was also available as a 3½-Litre, at £490. The engines were of 2663- and 3485-cc capacity respectively. Also offered were Saloon versions, as well as a 1½-Litre Saloon at £298.

1940

11A Standard Flying Eight

11B Standard Flying Eight

11A: **Standard** Flying Eight (or Flying Standard Eight) Drophead Coupé, restored and preserved by Mr Denis Redrupp of Selsdon, Surrey. In addition to this convertible model there was a Tourer which had smaller doors (with 'cut-out'), folding windscreen and simpler top. All Flying Eights had an 8·05 HP 1021-cc four-cylinder engine, driving through a three-speed gearbox.

11B: **Standard** Flying Eight was available with several body styles, but this type was not in the showrooms. It was one of a batch of nearly five hundred special canteen vans from which YMCA volunteers dispensed tea during the war years.

11C: **Standard** Flying Ten was one of a range of small and medium-sized cars, the others being the Flying Eight (*q.v.*), Nine, Twelve, Fourteen and Twenty. All models had four-cylinder side-valve engines except the Twenty, which had a Six. The Ten had a 9·99 HP 1267-cc engine, 7 ft 6 in wheelbase and cost £179. Body styling was fundamentally the same throughout the range but looked best on the larger models (see also 1946).

11C Standard Flying Ten

1940

page 12

12A: Standard Flying Twelve Drophead Coupé. This car had a 1608-cc engine, rated at 11·98 HP and a wheelbase of 8 ft 4 in. Compared with post-war production, the 1939/40 models had louvres in the bonnet sides. Front suspension was independent with transverse leaf spring.

12B: Sunbeam-Talbot Ten Saloon was an attractively styled four-seater with 9·8 HP 1185-cc engine and 7 ft 9 in wheelbase. It was a carry-over from 1939 and sold at £248. A Drophead Coupé variant was offered at £285.

12C: Sunbeam-Talbot 2-Litre Saloon was a larger edition of the Ten, with the same styling, but 3½-in longer wheelbase and 1944-cc 13·9 HP four-cylinder engine. 3- and 4-Litre models with six-cylinder power units were also offered. Only the Ten and the 2-Litre were continued after the war.

12A Standard Flying Twelve

12B Sunbeam-Talbot Ten

12C Sunbeam-Talbot 2-Litre

1940

13A Triumph Twelve

13B Triumph Twelve

13A: **Triumph** Twelve was introduced in 1939 at £285 and differed from the better-known Dolomites mainly in having more conventional front end styling and pressed steel wheels. The engine was an 11·8 HP 1496-cc (69 × 100 mm) and Triumph's 1767-cc engine was offered as optional. Wheelbase was 9 ft, tyre size 5.00-17. In 1940 the price was £313 10s.
13B: **Triumph** Twelve—one of a few of these rare cars still in existence. It is preserved by Mr F. R. Hebron of Blandford Forum, Dorset. Total production of Twelves was probably well under 50.
13C: **Triumph** Dolomite range comprised 13·95 HP 1767-cc Four (9 ft wb) and 15·7 HP 1991-cc Six (9 ft 8 in wb) models. All had 100-mm stroke, but cylinder bores were 75 and 65 mm respectively. They were carry-overs from 1939, with detail modifications. A four-cylinder Roadster is shown on page 14. At this time Triumph were in severe financial trouble and eventually went into liquidation. The Sheffield steel firm of Thomas W. Ward Ltd purchased the company from the Receiver in the autumn of 1939. A number of cars still in stock were disposed of by Wards, who also sold the various Coventry premises. The Gloria Works at Holbrooks Lane, for example, were bought by the Secretary of State for Air in February 1940, and the Stoke works were sold in November 1944, to the Standard Motor Co. Ltd, who subsequently reorganized the company as Triumph Motor Co. (1945) Ltd.

13C Triumph Dolomite Royal 14/60

1940

page 14

14 Triumph Dolomite Roadster (see page 13)

1940

15A: **Vauxhall** Ten, Series H, with two-door bodywork, selling at £163. The more common four-door Saloon cost £175. Both had a 9·99 HP 1203-cc OHV Four engine with three-speed gearbox and 7 ft 10 in wheelbase.

15B: **Vauxhall** Twelve, Series I, had basically the same styling as the Ten, but was of larger dimensions and had a wheelbase of 8 ft 5¼ in. The engine was a 1442-cc OHV Four of 11·98 HP and the saloon body was of the six-light type. Price was £198. A few more of these were produced in 1945–46 (*q.v.*).

15C: **Vauxhall** Fourteen, Series J, was in production during 1939–40 and continued after the war until 1948. It was larger than the Twelve, with 8 ft 9 in wheelbase, 5·50-16 tyres and 1781-cc six-cylinder engine of 14·07 HP. Price in 1940 was £235.

15A Vauxhall Ten

15B Vauxhall Twelve

15C Vauxhall Fourteen

1940

16A: **Wolseley** Ten, Series III, four-door Saloons in the Netherlands. The Ten was one of a wide range of cars offered by Nuffield's Wolseley Motors Ltd of Ward End, Birmingham. Others were the 12/48 four-cylinder and 14/60, 16/65, 18/85, 21 and 25 HP six-cylinder models, all with the same basic styling but varying in size and equipment. Prices were from £237 (Ten) up to £855 (25 Limousine).

16B: **Wolseley** Drophead Coupé on Special 25 HP Super Six chassis. The impressive front end featured large Lucas P100 headlamps, side lamps and twin flat-top-beam foglamps, as well as tuned Mellotone Post-Horns, operated by a loud/soft push in the steering-wheel centre. The 3485-cc OHV Six engine delivered 108 bhp and drove through a four-speed gearbox with synchromesh on 2nd, 3rd and top gears.

16A Wolseley Ten

16B Wolseley Super Six

1941–45

1941–45 With the exception of the last six months, 1941–45 was a period of almost total war production. Most of the truck manufacturers turned out military trucks of various types, whereas the car manufacturers were usually engaged in the production of totally different equipment. The main exceptions were Rootes (Hillman, Humber) and Standard. These companies produced large quantities of military cars and derivatives such as light trucks and light armoured cars, although they (and the truck industry) also turned out a variety of other items.

For a comprehensive coverage of vehicles produced for the Armed Forces, the reader is referred to *The Observer's Fighting Vehicles Directory, World War II* (Warne, 1972).

Most civilian car owners laid their vehicles up 'for the duration'. May 1945 saw the end of the war on the continent of Europe, and in the following August the Japanese surrendered. Production of vehicles, aircraft, etc., for the Services soon tailed off and the motor industry began gradually to revert to civilian work. Many 1939/40 models were reintroduced, usually incorporating detail modifications. These post-war cars are dealt with in the following section.

17A ATS vehicles

17B Aircraft production

17A: Typical line-up of vehicles operated by the ATS (Auxiliary Territorial Service), awaiting an inspection by the Princess Royal on 20 September 1941. The vehicles are, from left to right: Ariel W/NG motorcycle, Austin 8 HP Two-Seater, Humber Super Snipe and Ford WOA1 staff saloons, Ford 30 HP Utility, Austin 10 HP Light Utility and Morris-Commercial CS11/30F Heavy Ambulance. (IWM photo H14043). Some of the vehicles shown in this wartime section were already in production in 1939/40.

17B: The motor industry was engaged in several other forms of war material production, including aircraft. The picture shows the erecting hall of the Rootes-operated Airframe Factory at Speke, near Liverpool. The aircraft are Bristol Blenheim high-speed bombers for the RAF.

1941–45

18A Austin Ten

18B Austin Ten

18C Daimler Scout Car

18A: **Austin** Ten, Model GRQ, as used by the Forces, was a civilian saloon with a few modifications. The engine was a 9·99 HP 1125-cc side-valve Four of 29·5 bhp. The car was identical to the 1940 model, the only exception being that the gearbox third motion shaft flange was separate instead of integral with the shaft. From 1945 to 1947 it was continued as Model GS1. The car shown served with the RAF in the Far East.

18B: **Austin** Ten Light Utility, Model G/YG, was a modification of the Ten Saloon. It had two seats in the cab and two folding seats in the canvas-top rear body. Other notable differences when compared with the car were larger bore (66·65 v. 63·5 mm, resulting in 1237-cc capacity), addition of a water pump, lower gear ratios (final drive 6·14 v. 5·38 to 1), 8½- v. 6-gallon fuel tank and cross-country type tyres.

18C: **Daimler** automotive production during the war consisted mainly of Scout Cars (shown) and Armoured Cars. Total production figures were 6626 and 2694 respectively. The Scout Car, popularly known as the Daimler 'Dingo' (after a fast and rugged Australian dog), weighed about three tons. The 55-bhp 2·52-litre OHV engine, located at the rear, drove all four wheels through a fluid flywheel with pre-selective transmission. Two are shown here during a demonstration in Sheffield.

1941–45

19A Ford E83W

19C Ford W0A2

19D Ford W0A2

19B Ford W0A1

19A: **Ford** E83W 10-cwt Van, converted into Utilecon seven seater by Martin Walter Ltd. It had the 10 HP 1172-cc engine of the Prefect Saloon and a wheelbase of 7 ft 10 in. The Royal Navy and the Royal Air Force were among the users of the van and the conversion.

19B: **Ford** W0A1 staff car used the body of the pre-war Model 62 Saloon, but with a military pattern front end and 30 HP 85-bhp V8 engine. Tyre size was 9.00-13 or 6.50-16 (Model W0A1/A). During 1939–45, Ford Dagenham built about 360,000 fighting and transport vehicles to a total value of £138 million, and paid £25 million in wages and £12¾ million in taxes. (IWM photo E25140)

19C: **Ford** W0A2, Heavy Utility variant of the W0A1, was in production during 1941–44 and many remained in civilian use after the war. The vehicle shown is a now rare survivor, restored and preserved by Mr Bernard Venners, a military vehicle enthusiast in England.

19D: **Ford** W0A2 Tourer was a soft-top conversion of the Heavy Utility car. Such modifications, used mainly in North Africa, were also carried out on Humbers and Canadian Fords. (IWM photo NA2250)

1941–45

20 Ford WOA2 (after 'demob')

page 21

1941–45

21 Hillman Minx 10 HP (Royal Navy)

1941–45

22A: **Hillman** produced large numbers of Minx-based Light Utility 2 + 2-seaters, shown here with the canvas top removed. The two rear seats were of the folding type. There were several modifications for the many production contracts. This is an early model (Mk 1).

22B: **Hillman** 10 HP Light Utility, used in the Coventry Thanksgiving Week Procession on 13 October 1945. This is the final production type, featuring removable cab top and lifting sling flanges on the wheels.

22C: **Hillman** 10 HP Light Utility interior. Note the additional emergency seats at the extreme rear. This vehicle was one of many supplied to the Royal Air Force.

22A Hillman 10 HP

22B Hillman 10 HP

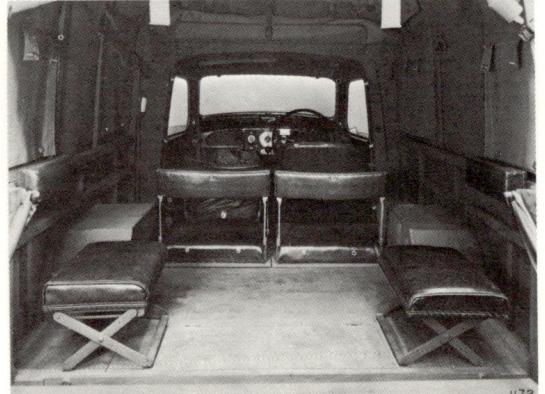

22C Hillman 10 HP

1941–45

23A Hillman 10 HP

23A: **Hillman** Convertible Van, used by the RAF, was another vehicle based on the Minx car. Basically it was similar to the Light Utility, but it had a van-type body with side windows and could be used for the transport of either personnel or goods. Another variant was the all-enclosed Ladder Van, fitted out for airfield lighting maintenance.

23B: **Hillman** 10 HP chassis with turreted armoured hull. This neat little armoured car, named Gnat, did not get beyond the experimental stage. The engine was mounted at the rear, the driver sitting in the forward end. Note the single headlamp, fitted with black-out mask.

23C: **Humber** Super Snipe Staff Saloon. This is a 1941 model which had larger tyres (9.00-13) and wider wings than the 1940 model (*q.v.*). It is shown in an Arab village during the Western Desert war in 1942. The windscreen was partly painted in order to minimize light reflection and detection from the air.

23B Hillman Gnat

23C Humber Super Snipe

1941–45

page 24

24 Humber Super Snipe ('Old Faithful' with Churchill, 'Monty', Alexander; Tripoli, Feb. 1943)

1941–45

25A: **Humber** Super Snipe Tourer was used extensively by Field Marshal Viscount Montgomery of Alamein. This picture was taken in 1952 when he paid a visit to the Coventry works of Rootes Motors Ltd, the parent company of Humber Ltd. Accompanied by Lord Rootes and Mr Geoffrey Rootes, he is touring the Stoke factory in one of his wartime cars, dubbed 'Old Faithful'. This car (M239459), which served the Field Marshal in North Africa and Italy, has been preserved.

25B: **Humber** Super Snipe Tourer No. M239485 was used by FM Montgomery during 1944/45 in Western Europe and became known as the 'Victory Car'. This car, like 'Old Faithful', was preserved. It is shown here during an inspection tour by Lord Montgomery, in August 1951, in the Castlemartin Army Training Area, Pembrokeshire.

25C: Another picture of a **Humber** Super Snipe Tourer, showing HM The Queen (then Princess) Elizabeth and Princess Margaret in King's Park, Edinburgh, in July 1946. The occasion was the commemoration of the 25th anniversary of the Scottish Branch of the British Legion.

25A Humber Super Snipe

25B Humber Super Snipe

25C Humber Super Snipe

1941–45

page 26

26A Humber Super Snipe

26C Humber Pullman

26B Humber Pullman

26A: **Humber** Super Snipe Heavy Utility was another variant on this widely used chassis. It was a military type estate car, used mainly by the Army and the RAF. This specimen was converted for wireless use and featured a canvas instead of metal roof. In one or two instances the complete top was removed, turning the car into a Tourer with folding canvas top. There was also an 8-cwt truck version with soft-top cab. Some of the latter were later fitted with staff saloon bodywork.

26B: **Humber** Pullman Limousines were used by high-ranking officers in the Army, RAF and RN. The bodywork was by Thrupp & Maberly and featured a glass partition behind the front seat and a roof luggage rail. Some had a wire mesh type radiator grille. The picture shows the production department at Thrupp & Maberly Ltd at Acton, in 1944.

26C: **Humber** Pullman Limousines were used also by the US Army. They were supplied under 'Reversed Lend-Lease'. This picture was taken in Normandy, in 1944.

1941–45

27A: **Humber** produced a large variety of 'soft-skin' and armoured military vehicles, using the same basic engine and other components throughout the range. Illustrated are a Pullman Limousine, a Special Ironside Saloon and a rear-engined 4 × 4 Armoured Car, Mark I, all part of the fleet of vehicles used by HM King George VI. The Pullman was one of three with special bullet-proof (austenitic steel) coachwork. In the background is Windsor Castle.

27B/C: **Humber** light armoured car, built on the Super Snipe chassis. Early models, produced for Home Defence following the Dunkirk evacuation, were known as Humberette. Illustrated is their follow-up, first produced in July 1940 and officially designated 'Car, 4 × 2, Light Reconnaissance, Humber Mk I, Ironside I'. It featured WD pattern divided-rim wheels with 9·25-16 Runflat tyres, and was superseded by the turreted Mk II and the four-wheel drive Mk III and IIIA. Altogether some 3600 were built.

27A Humber

27B Humber Ironside

27C Humber Ironside

1941–45

28A Humber Special Ironside

28B Humber Special Ironside

28C Humber Special Ironside

28A/B/C: **Humber** Special Ironside Saloons were used by the Royal Family and Cabinet Ministers. They were derived from the standard Ironside (q.v.) and had a division between front and rear compartment. The left-hand front seat back squab could be folded forward and the Perspex division panel moved to the right to facilitate access to the rear seat. Equipment in the rear compartment included an 8-day clock, a microphone to the driver, a wool rug and a fire extinguisher. Upholstery was hide, with West of England cloth on the sides, below waist level.

1941–45

29A Humber F.W.D.

29B Humber F.W.D.

29A: **Humber** F.W.D. chassis was derived from the Super Snipe but, as the model designation indicates, featured four-wheel drive. The chassis was used for utility cars, armoured reconnaissance cars and 8-cwt trucks and field ambulances. In addition to the conventional four-speed gearbox, it had a two-speed auxiliary gearbox, providing eight forward and two reverse speeds. Front suspension was independent.

29B: **Humber** four-wheel drive (4 × 4) Heavy Utility car under test, negotiating a deep mud and water course at 30 mph. These cars weighed almost 2½ tons.

29C: **Humber** Heavy Utility and Light Reconnaissance Car, Mk III, in the North African desert. Both used the same four-wheel drive chassis with 9 ft 3¾ in wheelbase and 9·25-16 tyres.

29C Humber F.W.D.

1941–45

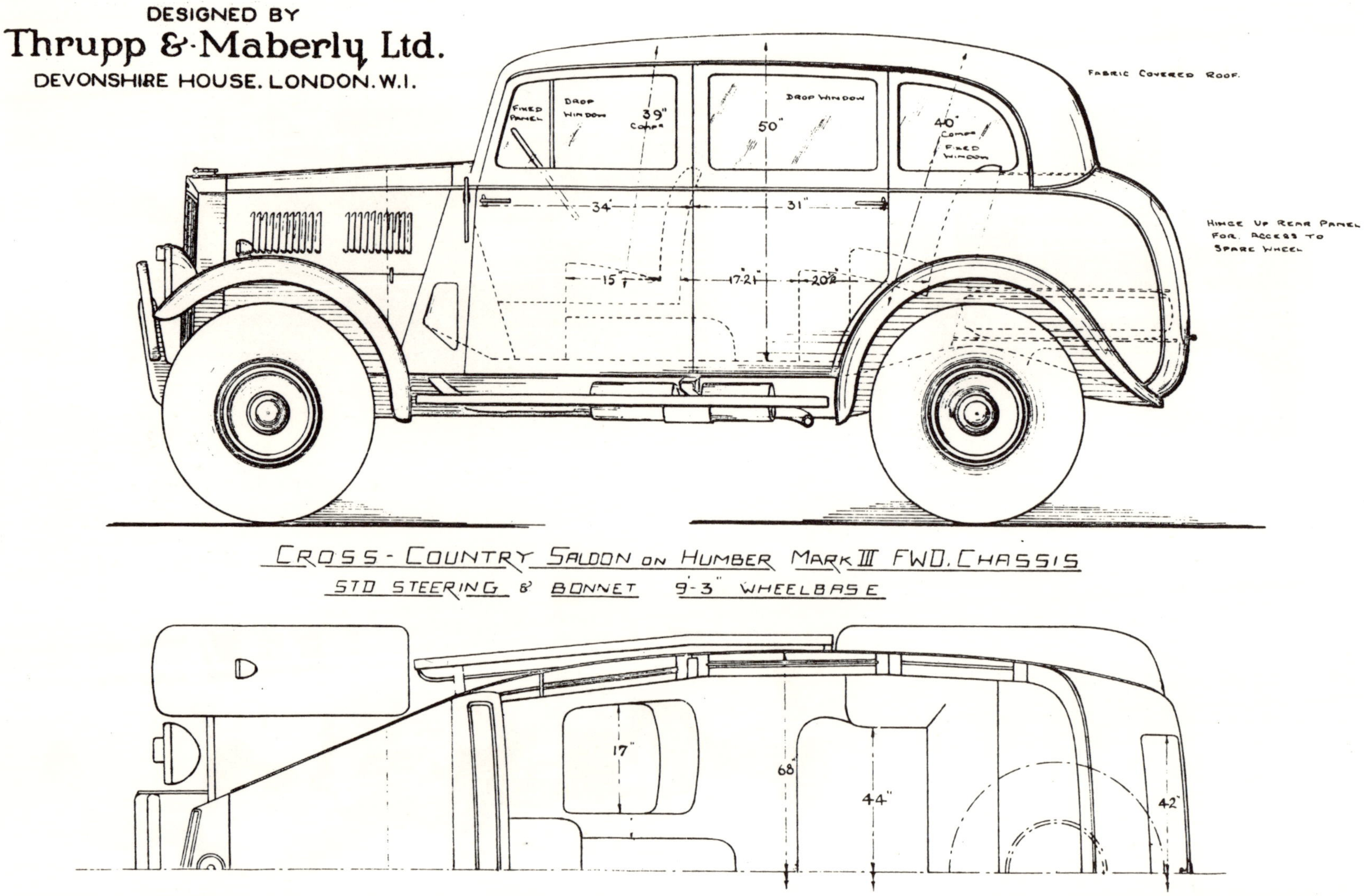

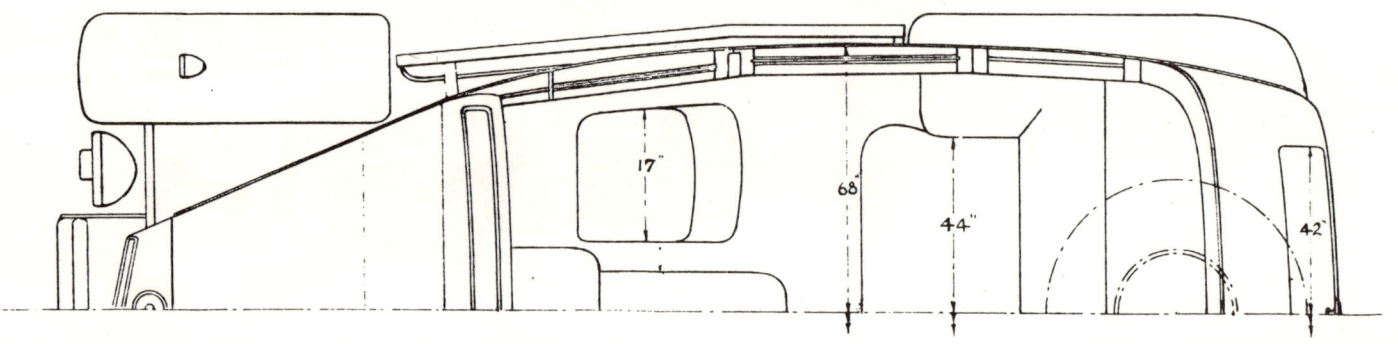

30 Humber F.W.D. Staff Saloon

1941–45

30: **Humber** F.W.D. cross-country chassis with special four-seater saloon bodywork designed by Thrupp & Maberly Ltd in 1943. It used the standard chassis and front end, and featured a fabric covered roof. It is uncertain whether any were actually produced. A soft-top Tourer variant was also designed, with bodywork similar to that of the Super Snipe Tourer (except for six seats and folding windscreen).

31A Humber F.W.D.

31B Humber Scout Car

31A: **Humber** F.W.D. Heavy Utility after 'demob'. Many remained in military service until long after the war; others found their way to 'Civvy Street'. These smartly turned out examples were used by the BBC (who, during the war, employed a conversion of the ambulance version on this chassis as recording vans for use in battle zones).

31B: **Humber** Scout Car was a rear-engined four-wheel drive armoured vehicle, using many of the components of the front-engined Humber F.W.D. vehicles. Some 4300 were produced during 1942–45 to supplement the Daimler 'Dingo' (q.v.), the production of which could not keep up with the demand. The Humber was larger (crew 3 v. 2) than the Daimler and less sophisticated. It had a fixed roof with sliding hatches and a Bren machine gun was mounted on top. Another supplementary source for scout cars was Ford of Canada (Ford Lynx).

1941–45

32A Morris 8 HP

32B Morris 10 HP

32A: **Morris** 8 HP Light Utility was based on the pre-war GPO van. Few were made, most Morris Light Utility cars being of the 10 HP type (q.v.).
32B: **Morris** 10 HP Light Utility vehicles on the assembly line at Cowley, Oxford. These are early production models, still featuring the civilian type radiator grille and headlamps.
32C: **Morris** 10 HP Light Utility was basically similar to those produced by Austin and Hillman, but based on the Morris Ten Saloon, Series M, of 1939/40. Technical differences compared with the car included a Solex carburettor (instead of SU), repositioning of the water pump (in front of the cylinder head instead of on the cylinder block), lower gear ratios, etc. It is shown here in an advertisement which appeared shortly after D-Day.

Dunkirk—and after!

Alan Moorehead, the famous War Correspondent, writing from the Beachhead—June 12

"It must have been pleasant for General Montgomery to see among our booty a number of British vehicles of the Morris make which the Germans apparently captured at Dunkirk and are still using."

—Testimony to the reliability of Morris Cars

MORRIS

A NUFFIELD PRODUCT

32C Morris 10 HP

1941–45

33B Nuffield/Willys

33C Nuffield

33A Morris LRC Mk I

33A: **Morris** Light Reconnaissance Cars were built in Mk I (4 × 2) and Mk II (4 × 4) versions, both with the engine at the rear. The former had IFS. The engine was a Morris EK four-cylinder petrol unit of 3·52-litre cubic capacity, producing 71 bhp, driving through a four-speed main gearbox and a two-speed transfer case. 2200 were produced, for the Army and the RAF.

33B: **Nuffield** Mechanizations Ltd, one of the divisions of The Nuffield Organization, were deeply involved in army mechanization projects during the 1930s and 1940s. About 1944 the company produced this experimental lightweight two-seater for airborne use. The major mechanical components were of Willys ('Jeep') manufacture; everything else was redesigned for compactness and reduced weight. The steering column was easily removable, and the top and windscreen could be folded down.

33C: **Nuffield** field car which did eventually reach the production stage, although in different form. It was what became known as 'Gutty' (later 'Mudlark' and eventually, when in quantity production, the Austin-built 'Champ'). Work on this project commenced during the war under the direction of Mr (later Sir) Alec Issigonis. The car, of which an artist's impression is shown, featured a stressed-skin welded steel body, four-wheel drive and torsion bar independent suspension.

1941–45

34A SS VA

34B SS VA

34A/B/C: **SS** Cars Ltd (later Jaguar) produced this prototype Ultra Lightweight car in 1943. It was powered by a V-twin 1096-cc JAP engine, driving through a lockable differential, and was intended as a possible replacement for the motorcycle with sidecar combination. Following unsatisfactory test results, the project was soon abandoned. Shown lifting the car is Mr W. T. F. (Wally) Hassan, one of the designers, who remained with Jaguar Cars Ltd until his retirement in 1972. Mr Hassan, as engineering director, was a key man in the development of many Jaguar designs, including the current V12 engine.

34C SS VA

page 34

1941–45

35A SS VB

35B SS VB

35A/B: **SS** Cars' second prototype, designated VB, was of more conventional design than the Model VA. It was powered by a Ford Ten engine, driving through a Ford three-speed gearbox plus a two-speed 'booster gear'. Both the VA and VB had independent suspension and rear wheel drive only. The rear suspension of the VB was of the same basic configuration as that of the much later Jaguar E-Type.
35C: **SS** VB Ultra Lightweight vehicle, side elevation. The top was of the folding type and the steering-wheel easily removable for ease of air transport. The VB, like the VA, remained in the experimental stage.

35C SS VB

1941–45

36 Standard 'Jungle Bug'

1941–45

37A: **Standard** also produced some Ultra Lightweight vehicles, in 1944, for possible military use. They were powered by a modified Standard Eight engine with magneto ignition. There were motorcycle-type saddles and pillions for the driver and three passengers. Vehicle shown, the first, had rear-wheel drive only.

37B: **Standard** JAB (Jungle Airborne Buggy), a development of the earlier 4 × 2 type, was more sophisticated and had four-wheel drive through a single-speed transfer case which was bolted to the Standard Eight type aluminium alloy engine/gearbox unit. The vehicles were intended for airborne operations in the jungles of the Far East, but did not see active service.

37C: **Standard** JAB Mk II had several modifications, including redesigned wings. Only about six of these vehicles were built and at least two have survived. One of these was later fitted with a Triumph Mayflower engine and a bench-type front seat replaced the original saddles. The front axle drive casing was cast as an integral unit with the engine sump. The tyres were 7.50-10, a special aero tyre, modified to have cross-country tread. Also seen here is an amphibious trailer into which the front end of the vehicle was to be placed, for ferrying across rivers. During the first test, in a water tank, the outfit sank straight to the bottom. Afterwards, four empty Jerry cans were fixed to the rear corners of the trailer for extra buoyancy.

37A Standard 'Jungle Bug'

37B Standard JAB

37C Standard JAB

1941–45

38A/B: **Standard** FGPV (Farmers' General Purpose Vehicle) was developed from the Model JAB 4 × 4 (*q.v.*) in 1944/45 and intended for civilian use after the war. As can be seen it was not unlike the SS VB, and both were clearly mini-versions of the US 'Jeep'. The FGPV was expected to sell at between £100 and £140, but the project did not materialize.

38C: **Standard** 12 HP 'Car, 5-cwt, 4 × 2, WVEE 493' was more like the 'Jeep' and a good-looking job. It had a wheelbase of 75 inches and turned the scales at 19 cwt. Built in 1943, it was fractionally lighter and smaller than the 'Jeep', but did not reach the quantity production stage, probably because Lend-Lease supply of 'Jeeps' was maintained at a higher rate than anticipated.

38A Standard FGPV

38B Standard FGPV

38C Standard 12 HP

1941–45

39A Standard 14 HP

39B Standard 20 HP

39A: **Standard** 14 HP 12-cwt Van of the Royal Air Force. Like the later Light Utility models, this vehicle had a beam-type front axle, unlike a 10-cwt version (also for the RAF) which had the 12 HP engine, 8 ft 4 in (v. 9 ft) wheelbase and independent front suspension. Van shown has forward end of saloon; others had a rather square cab and a wire-mesh radiator grille.
39B: **Standard** Flying Twenty chassis with ambulance bodywork and canvas top cab. This 20 HP chassis, which was not to be continued after the war, differed from the 14 HP in having a six-cylinder engine of 2664-cc and 9 ft 8 in (v. 9 ft) wheelbase. Bore and stroke were the same as for the four-cylinder 14 HP, namely 73 × 106 mm. As can be seen, the bonnet was slightly longer. The RAF used similar ambulances on the 14 HP chassis, for domestic use. Their bodywork and finish, however, were more austere.

1941–45

page 40

40A Standard 12 HP

40B Standard 12 HP

40C Standard 12 HP

40A/B: **Standard** 12 HP Light Utility as produced for the RAF. This edition (1942) used the front end sheet metal and the transverse-leaf independent front suspension of the civilian 12 HP Saloon. There was also a 10-cwt Van on this chassis. The front view shown is that of a preserved specimen restored by Mr Clive Sarjantson of Crowthorne, Berkshire.

40C: **Standard** 12 HP Light Utility as produced for the British Army. This model had a rigid front axle with longitudinal leaf springs and a wire-mesh radiator grille. The Standard had a military pattern cab, unlike the Austin and Hillman Light Utilities which are also seen in this picture. These are three vehicles of the Groombridge Collection, in the 1972 London to Brighton Run of the Historic Commercial Vehicle Club.

1941–45

41A: **Standard**, at the beginning of the war, produced a number of improvised light armoured cars on their 14 HP car chassis with beam-type front axle. The armour consisted of 11-mm mild steel, backed by 3-inch thick oak planks at the front. The hull was open-topped (and open-backed on the Mk I) and the vehicles, named after their instigator Lord Beaverbrook, were used for the defence of aircraft factories and for training purposes. Wheelbase was 9 ft, weight 2 tons. A Bren gun could be fired through vertical slots, front and rear.

41B/C: **Standard** Beaverette III and IV were produced when supplies of proper armour plate became available. The armour was 10 mm thick, and was bolted and welded together to form a turreted 'mobile pillbox'. One post-war civilian owner spent a lot of time and money cutting the hull down to resemble that of a field car (41B), and in 1971/72 Mr Cyril Groombridge of Heathfield, Sussex, very courageously reversed the process and restored the vehicle to what it looked like originally. The car is shown here before and after the extensive rebuild.

41A Standard Beaverette II

41B Standard Beaverette IV

41C Standard Beaverette IV

1941–45

42A Wolseley

42B Buick

42A: **Wolseley** mobile canteen, operated by the Salvation Army and paid for by the Christian Science War Relief Committee. This is just one example of hundreds of wartime conversions of pre-war cars.
42B: Heavy and powerful American cars were particularly suitable for conversion into boxvan-type canteens, ambulances, fire service control rooms, etc. A typical example of an ambulance body by Park Ward replacing the cut-off rear body of a 1936 Canadian-built Buick is shown here. Excessive rear overhang caused problems when lighter chassis were used.

1946

1946 The war hardly over, car manufacturers wasted no time in reverting to civilian production. Most cars were carry-overs from 1939/40, but there were some new models as will be seen in the following pages. Newly produced cars in 1945 were at first delivered only to essential users; later they could be acquired only against a permit issued by the Ministry of War Transport. The basic ration of petrol was restored, enabling pleasure motoring to be resumed on a basis of about 200 miles per month. New car prices were high and included the new Purchase Tax. Faced with the urgent need for stimulating export, the Government required the motor industry to export half of their production of cars and one-third of new commercial vehicles. Cars, buses and trucks could be sold almost anywhere, particularly in war-torn Western Europe. North America was ready for large numbers of sports cars, and firms such as MG could not produce enough to meet the demand. Car production in 1945 and 1946 totalled 16,938 and 219,162 respectively. By the beginning of 1946 some 1½ million cars were in use in the UK.

43A Headquarters of the SMM & T

43A: The headquarters of the British Motor Industry, 148 Piccadilly, London, W1, decorated for the Motor Industry's Jubilee celebrations. These premises, occupied by the Society of Motor Manufacturers and Traders, were officially opened by the Rt. Hon. John Wilmot MP, Minister of Supply, on 18 July 1946. He also opened the Jubilee Exhibition, which was housed in the same building.
43B: Typical traffic scene in 1946. The building is Devonshire House, Piccadilly, London, W1, during the Jubilee celebrations. Cars include 1938 Rolls-Royce, Wolseley, Ford and Hudson.

43B Piccadilly in 1946

1946

ALLARD

4-Seater open sports.

In the post-war Allard there is found the reliable large capacity, multi-cylinder engine capable of many thousands of miles without attention and the good ground clearance characteristic of the American car; the light-weight chassis, independent front suspension, excellent road holding and streamlining of the Continental car; and the first-class workmanship, excellent body work, powerful brakes, comfortable seating and safety typical of the best British cars.

In addition to all these the Allard has an exceptional power/weight ratio never before available with reliability, modest petrol consumption and freedom from an extensive maintenance.

4-seater Coupé

4-seater Saloon

Competition 2-seater

A catalogue giving full details is available on request.

ALLARD MOTOR COMPANY LIMITED, 43, ACRE LANE, LONDON, S.W.2.
BRIXTON 6431.

44A Allard L

44B Alvis Fourteen

44A: **Allard** cars were powered by developed versions of the well-known Ford V8 3·6-litre engine. Shown in this advertisement is the Model L open four-seater, which had a wheelbase of 9 ft 4 in. Sydney Allard was a well-known participant in pre-war trials and speed events, using Ford-based Specials of his own design. Quantity production of post-war Allard cars commenced in 1946, and during the ensuing years a large variety was produced, many finding their way to North America in chassis form (to be fitted with Cadillac and other V8 engines). The body design was partly the work of Godfrey Imhof, another well-known rally and trials driver.

44B: **Alvis** Fourteen TA14 Saloon was the Company's only model in production during 1946. It was a new and beautifully proportioned four-door four-light model, powered by a four-cylinder 1892-cc (74 × 110 mm) OHV engine, driving through a four-speed gearbox. Wheelbase was 9 ft, tyre size 6.00-16.

1946

45C Austin Sixteen

45A: **Armstrong Siddeley** started post-war production in November 1945 with the 16 HP Lancaster Saloon (shown) and Hurricane Drophead Coupé, supplemented by the Typhoon Two-door Saloon from August 1946. They remained in production until September 1949, when the engine was uprated. 1945–49 models had a 1991-cc (65 × 100 mm) 70-bhp OHV power unit. Wheelbase was 9 ft 7 in, tyre size 5.50-17. Pre-production Lancaster and Hurricane cars had made their debut as early as May 1945—during the same week as VE Day (Victory in Europe).

45B: **Austin** Tens, as well as Eight and Twelve, were reintroduced in 1945 with various improvements. Many of the changes were a result of wartime modifications to the Ten Light Utility which had been in almost continuous production during 1941–44. Basically, however, all three cars were much the same as in 1939/40. This advertisement appeared in the motoring press as early as February 1945.

45B Austin Ten

45A Armstrong Siddeley Lancaster

45C: **Austin** Sixteen, Model BS1, was new in the Company's immediate post-war programme. This car was basically the same as the Twelve (HS1), but instead of a 1535-cc side-valve engine it had a new 2199-cc overhead-valve unit with an output of 58 bhp at 3700 rpm. The RAC rating was 15·99 HP. Automatic reversing light, built-in hydraulic jacks and heater were standard equipment on the Sixteen. The saloon illustrated was delivered to the RAF. Post-war production of the 8, 10, 12 and 16 HP Saloons started in August 1945 and ceased in October 1947, with the exception of the 16 HP, which was continued until early 1949. In June 1946, the millionth car came off Austin's Longbridge assembly line. It was a Sixteen, finished in matt cream.

1946

46A: **Bentley** post-war production commenced in May 1946, with the Mark VI Saloon. Other body styles were also offered, as well as the bare chassis for specialist coachwork. The engine was a six-cylinder F-head (overhead inlet, side exhaust) 29·4 HP unit of 4257-cc cubic capacity with twin SU carburettors and four-speed gearbox. Wheelbase was 10 ft, tyre size 6.50-16. It was continued in this form until September 1951, when a larger bore 4566-cc engine was introduced.

46B: **Daimler** 2½-Litre, Model DB18, was introduced in February 1946. It was available in chassis form, with drophead coupé bodywork and as a four-door saloon (shown). The engine was a 2522-cc 70-bhp OHV Six, driving through a fluid flywheel and pre-selector epicyclic gearbox and worm drive rear axle. Front suspension was independent with coil springs.

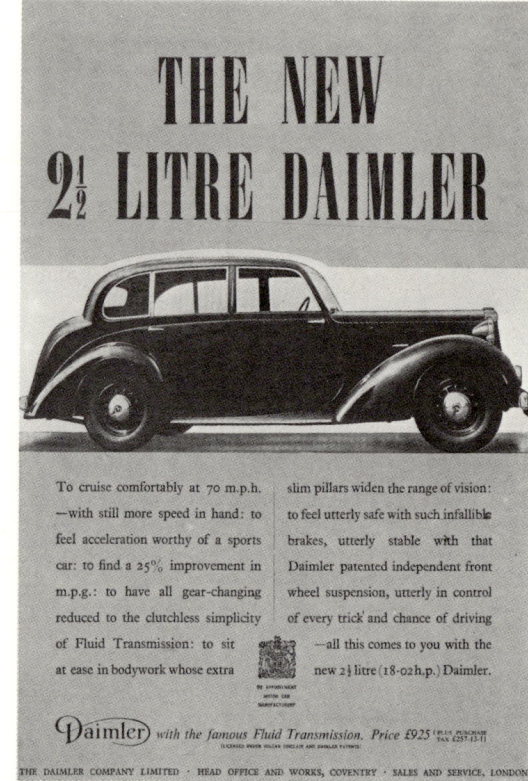

46A Bentley 4¼-Litre Mark VI

46B Daimler 2½-Litre

46C: **Daimler** Straight Eight, Model DE36, was available in chassis and Limousine form. It was the largest Daimler available and the eight-cylinder 5460-cc engine had the same cylinder dimensions (85·09 × 120 mm) as the 4095-cc six-cylinder Model DE27. Both were OHV engines, with twin SU carburettors, producing 110 and 150 bhp respectively. Front suspension was independent, wheelbase 12 ft 3 in and 11 ft 6½ in respectively. Production started in March.

46C Daimler Straight Eight

page 47

1946

47A: **Ford** Anglia 8 HP, Model E04A, was a carry-over from 1939/40 albeit with some detail improvements and modifications. Post-war production started in October 1945. The four-cylinder side-valve engine was of 933-cc capacity, having a bore and stroke of 56·6 × 92·5 mm. With 6·3:1 CR it developed 23·4 bhp. Gearbox was three-speed, wheelbase 7 ft 6 in, tyre size 4.50-17. It remained virtually unchanged until late in 1948.

47B: **Ford** Prefect 10 HP, Model E93A, was also put into production in October 1945. It was fundamentally the same as produced in 1939/40 and differed from the Anglia chiefly in the following respects: four-door bodywork with different front and rear end, 7 ft 10 in wheelbase, 12 ft 11¼ in (v. 12 ft 8¼ in) overall length, 5.00-16 tyres and 63·5-mm cylinder bore, giving 1172-cc cubic capacity. Maximum power output, with 6·16:1 CR, was 30 bhp. The millionth vehicle to emerge from Ford's Dagenham plant (opened in 1931) was a white Prefect, in August 1946. It was driven from the assembly line by the Minister of Supply, Mr John Wilmot.

47A Ford Anglia

47B Ford Prefect

47C: **Frazer-Nash-Bristol** 2-Litre was announced in 1946, although quantity production did not commence until 1947, by which time it was known as the Bristol 400. The car was developed by the Bristol Aeroplane Company in conjunction with Messrs Adlington of AFN Ltd, producers of the Frazer-Nash-BMW. The latter was basically the pre-war German BMW 328, and the engine of the new car was developed by Bristol during 1945–46, also from the BMW 328. It was a 1971-cc OHV Four with three SU carburettors. The new car had a well-streamlined four-seater body on a massive-looking but light box girder frame, with a wheelbase of 9 ft 6 in, IFS with transverse leaf spring and torsion bar rear springing.

47C Frazer-Nash-Bristol 2-Litre

1946

page 48

48A Hillman Minx

48B Hillman Minx

48A: **Hillman** Minx as reintroduced in 1945 had, it was claimed, no fewer than 57 improvements compared with the 1940 model, to which it looked identical. The price, in October 1946, was £442 and a Drophead Coupé was available at £525, both prices inclusive of PT.
48B: **Hillman** Minx Estate Car, a derivation of the van. Hillman Minx-based vans carried the Commer nameplate, Commer being the principal line of Rootes' commercial vehicles.
48C: **HRG** offered two Sports Two-Seaters, the 1074-cc 1100 and the 1496-cc 1500 (shown). They were similar in appearance, but apart from the 44- and 61-bhp engines, differed slightly in dimensions, the wheelbase being 8 ft $4\frac{1}{2}$ in and 8 ft $7\frac{1}{2}$ in respectively. Both engines were based on Singer units, with overhead camshaft and twin SU carburettors. The cars were made in small numbers by HRG Engineering Co. in Tolworth, Surrey.

48C HRG 1500

1946

49A: **Humber** post-war range comprised three five-seater saloons: the new 14 HP Hawk, the 18 HP Snipe and the 27 HP Super Snipe. In addition there was the seven-passenger 27 HP Pullman Limousine. Shown is a Super Snipe, belonging to Sir Graham and Lady Cunningham. This model, fundamentally the same as in 1940, was known as the Super Snipe Mark I. It had a 100-bhp 4-litre side-valve six-cylinder engine and was in production from August 1945 to September 1948.

49A Humber Super Snipe

49B: **Humber** Super Snipe with attractive Estate Car coachwork. This was not a regular production body style but a special vehicle bodied by Thrupp & Maberly. Note the 'boot scrapers' below the doors.

49B Humber Super Snipe

1946

page 50

50A Humber Pullman

50B Humber Pullman

50A: **Humber** Pullman was mechanically similar to the Super Snipe, but had 12-in v. 11-in Lockheed hydraulic brakes and 10 ft 7½ in v. 9 ft 6 in wheelbase. It could carry seven passengers and driver. The 4-litre side-valve Six engine developed 100 bhp at 3400 rpm. All Humbers had IFS with wishbones and transverse leaf spring.

50B/51: **Humber** Pullman with special luxurious Sedanca De Ville coachwork built to special order by H. J. Mulliner & Co. Ltd, for Rootes Ltd. With the main exception of the radiator grille, all the bodywork was different from the regular Pullman Limousine. It is shown here with the front compartment roof section removed and installed. *The Motor* wrote 'The bodywork is a good example of compromise between British and American styling, the car having flowing lines without over-exaggeration'. The price of the car was £2300, plus PT (November 1946).

page 51

1946

51 Humber Pullman Sedanca De Ville by Mulliner

1946

52A: **Jaguar** Cars Ltd (formerly SS Cars Ltd, a name changed for obvious reasons) re-entered the post-war market with basically unchanged 1½-, 2½- and 3½-Litre Sports Saloons. There were several detail improvements. Except for certain features of equipment, the same style of coachwork was used for all three cars. The 1½-Litre was a Four (73 × 106 mm); the others were Sixes (73 × 106 and 82 × 110 mm), all with OHV.

52B: **Jensen** Straight Eight Saloon was a beautifully-styled high-performance car intended for the luxury market. The engine was a 130-bhp 3860-cc (85 × 85 mm) 36·5 HP OHV 8-in-line with two SU carburettors, driving through an overdrive-top four-speed gearbox. Although announced in the summer of 1946, it was not until early 1948 that series production actually got under way. This advertisement appeared in September 1946.

52C: **Jowett** Javelin was first announced in mid-1946 and went into quantity production in the following year. It was an entirely new car, bristling with unusual design features. The horizontally-opposed four-cylinder water-cooled OHV engine was mounted ahead of the front wheel axis. It was of 1486-cc cubic capacity (72·5 × 90 mm) and with a CR of 7·25:1 and two Zenith carburettors produced 50 bhp. Top speed was nearly 80 mph, fuel consumption averaging between 25–30 mpg. Drive was to the rear wheels via a steering column-controlled four-speed gearbox and divided propeller shaft.

52A Jaguar 2½/3½-Litre

52B Jensen Straight Eight

52C Jowett Javelin

1946

53A: **Lanchester** Ten, Series LD10, was produced from February 1946 until July 1951, although 1950/51 models had restyled bodywork (four-light, by Barker). The engine, a 40-bhp OHV Four of 1287 cc, was one of the most powerful Tens of the day. It drove through a fluid flywheel with pre-selector gearbox. Wheelbase was 8 ft 3 in, tyre size 5.25-16.

53B: **Lea-Francis** 12 and 14 HP models of 1946 were similar in principle to the pre-war cars but considerably modified in detail. In addition to the four-light Saloon (shown) there was a Utility/estate car. A Coupé was added early in 1947 and a short-wheelbase Sports model in 1948. 12 and 14 had 100-mm stroke and 69- and 75-mm bore respectively, giving 1496- and 1767-cc cubic capacity. Both were OHV Fours with two high-positioned camshafts and hemi-spherical combustion chambers. 1947 saloons had deeper side windows, whereby the 'upper waistline' was eliminated

53C: **Lea-Francis** chassis was underslung at the rear and had 9 ft 3 in wheelbase and 5.50-17 tyres. Suspension was conventional with rigid axles and semi-elliptic leaf springs front and rear. Brakes were Girling mechanical.

53A Lanchester Ten

53B Lea-Francis 12 & 14 HP

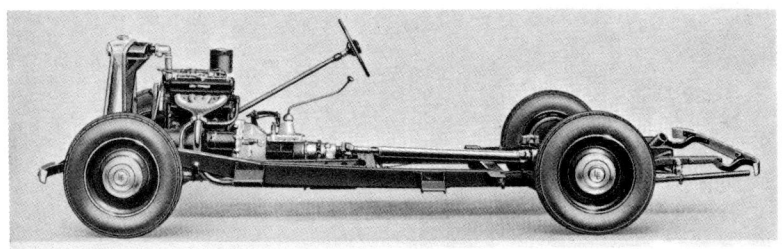

53C Lea-Francis 12 & 14 HP

1946

54A: **MG** Midget TC was produced from November 1945 until December 1949, during which period the impressive total of about 10,000 was made. A large proportion of these were exported, notably to North America. The TC resembled the 1939 TB in all but relatively minor respects. The body was four inches wider, the instrumentation was revised, a new synchromesh gearbox was fitted and the roadsprings had shackles rather than the previous sliding trunnions. Engine was 54·4-bhp 1250-cc four-cylinder with twin SUs. Wheelbase was 7 ft 10 in, tyre size 4.50-19.

54B: **Morgan** F-4 was a four-seater three-wheeler with 933-cc 22-bhp four-cylinder side-valve Ford Eight engine. Transmission was by shaft from flywheel through centre bearing (obviating shaft whip) to three-speed gearbox, thence to worm and wheel with single-chain final drive. Wheelbase was 8 ft 3 in, basic price £235 (August 1946).

54C: **Morgan** F Super was basically similar to the F-4 but with shortened wheelbase (7 ft 11 in), 1172-cc Ford Ten engine and two-seater bodywork. It had a maximum speed of over 70 mph and could cruise at 65 mph. The basic price was £260.

54D: **Morgan** 4/4 Drophead Coupé had a 38·8-bhp 1267-cc OHV four-cylinder engine, specially made by the Standard Motor Co. and rated at 9·99 HP. The gearbox had four speeds and Girling brakes were fitted. The two-seater bodywork had luggage accommodation inside the folding hood; the car carried two spare wheels. Wheelbase was 7 ft 8 in, overall height 4 ft 3 in. A two-seater Roadster and four-seater Tourer were also offered.

54A MG Midget TC

54B Morgan F-4

54C Morgan F Super

54D Morgan Drophead Coupé

1946

55A: Morris 1946 models were carry-overs from 1939/40 and comprised Eight, Series E, two- and four-door Saloons and Ten four-door Saloons, all with fixed or sliding roof. Illustrated is a four-door Eight with sliding roof, which was priced at £300 plus just over £84 PT. Post-war production of the Eight had commenced in October 1945, in two-door form, the four-door being added in January 1946. Both had 7 ft 5 in wheelbase, 4.50-17 tyres.

55B: Morris Ten, Series M, was reintroduced in September 1945, although it had been in production during the war years in military Light Utility form. The car was available only with four doors, with or without a sliding roof. Engine capacity was 1140 cc (Eight: 918·6 cc), maximum brake horsepower 37·2 (Eight: 29·6). Unlike the Eight, the Ten had overhead valves. Suspension was conventional with longitudinal leaf springs all round. Wheelbase was 7 ft 10 in, tyre size 5.00-16. Later in the year a new rounded radiator grille was introduced. This model was also produced in India, named Hindustan.

55C: Riley introduced an entirely new and most attractive post-war model in September 1945. The engine was not much different from that of the pre-war 1½-Litre. The new chassis featured Torsionic IFS with torsion bars and the body, too, was of an entirely new design. In October 1946, a 2½-Litre model was added which had a longer bonnet and a pale blue instead of a dark blue radiator badge. Cubic capacities of the engines were 1496 and 2443 cc respectively. Wheelbase was 9 ft 4½ in for the 1½-Litre, 9 ft 11 in for the 2½-Litre.

55A Morris Eight

55B Morris Ten

55C Riley 1½-Litre

1946

56A Rolls-Royce Silver Wraith

56B Rover Twelve

56C Rover Fourteen

56A: **Rolls-Royce** Silver Wraith 4¼-Litre, produced during 1946–51, had a six-cylinder 4257-cc (88·89 × 114·3 mm) 29·4 HP 126-bhp engine with twin-choke Stromberg carburettor and 6·4:1 CR. It had overhead inlet and side exhaust valves (F-head type). Gearbox was four-speed, wheelbase 10 ft 7 in. Several body styles were offered.

56B: **Rover** offered Ten, Twelve, Fourteen and Sixteen Saloons. The latter three were also available with Sports Saloon bodywork (Twelve shown). This body style was a little less in height and had four side windows instead of six, providing a more lengthy appearance. The Twelve had a 1496-cc OHV Four engine and 9 ft 4 in wheelbase.

56C: **Rover** Fourteen Saloon with six-light bodywork. It was similar to the Sixteen, the main exception being the cubic capacity of the six-cylinder OHV engines, 1901 and 2174 cc respectively. Model shown cost £812, as four-light Sports Saloon £831.

1946

57A Singer Nine

57B Singer Super Ten

57C Standard Eight

57D Standard Eight

57A: **Singer** Nine Roadster appeared in May 1946. It had aluminium-panelled four-seater bodywork, a 1074-cc (60 × 95 mm) OHC engine with one SU carburettor, three-speed gearbox and 7 ft 7 in wheelbase. It was continued until late in 1949, when a Solex carburettor, a four-speed gearbox and other detail modifications were introduced. Price £493.

57B: **Singer** Super Ten went into production in December 1945, and had an 1193-cc (63·25 × 95 mm) 37-bhp OHC engine. In December 1946 the Super Twelve Saloon was added. It was similar to the Super Ten, but somewhat larger, and powered by a 43-bhp 1525-cc (68 × 105 mm) engine, also with overhead camshaft. Wheelbase sizes were 7 ft 11 in and 8 ft 7 in respectively.

57C: **Standard** Eight Saloon was substantially similar to the 1940 model, the main external difference being the omission of the louvres in the bonnet sides. A minor modification was that the transverse leaf spring of the front suspension was now anchored with six instead of four bolts. Also, the three-speed gearbox was replaced by a four-speed.

57D: **Standard** Eight Tourer. A Drophead Coupé was also offered. The latter had wind-up windows and no door cut-outs.

1946

58A Standard Twelve

58B Standard Twelve

58C Standard Fourteen

58A: **Standard** Twelve Utility. This model was produced for export and was based on the military 12 HP chassis with beam type front axle and semi-elliptic leaf springs (the only post-war Standard car without IFS). It also retained the rectangular military type instrument panel, set in a wooden dash panel. Below the rear window was a small bottom-hinged door, providing access to the loading space behind the (folding) rear seat. This door lid, when left open, formed a strong platform for long or additional loads.

58B: **Standard** Twelve Drophead Coupé. This 1609-cc 11·98 HP chassis was also produced with four-door saloon bodywork, identical to that of the Fourteen (*q.v.*).

58C: **Standard** Fourteen Saloon (shown) and Drophead Coupé were generally similar to the corresponding Twelve models but had a larger-bore 1776-cc 13·23 HP engine. Prices were the same, £479 for the Saloons, £505 for the Coupés.

1946

59A Sunbeam-Talbot Ten

59B Sunbeam-Talbot 2-Litre

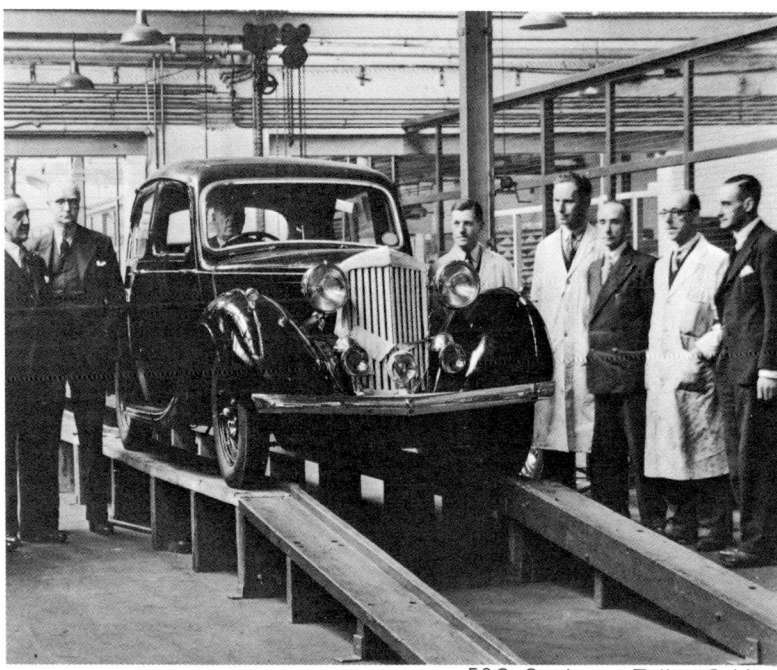

59C Sunbeam-Talbot 2-Litre

59A: **Sunbeam-Talbot** Ten Saloon was same as in 1940 except for detail improvements including redesigned aluminium cylinder head. The 1185-cc 41-bhp side-valve Four engine (derived from the Hillman Minx) drove through a four-speed gearbox and the Bendix Duo-Servo brakes were cable-operated. A Sports Tourer and a Drophead Coupé were also available. Prices were £684, £646 and £729 respectively (including PT).

59B: **Sunbeam-Talbot** 2-Litre Sports Tourer, previously owned by Mr Douglas Clease, winner of the French Alpine Trial. The 2-Litre models (Saloon, Tourer and Drophead Coupé) had a 1944-cc 56-bhp four-cylinder side-valve engine and 10-in Lockheed hydraulic brakes. Both the Ten and the 2-Litre were in production from July 1945 to June 1948.

59C: **Sunbeam-Talbot** production was transferred by Rootes, the parent company, to Ryton-on-Dunsmore, near Coventry. This was the last car to come off the assembly line of the old Barlby Road, London, works, on 31 May 1946.

1946

60A Triumph 1800

60B Triumph 1800

60A: **Triumph** Motor Co. Ltd was taken over by Standard (*see* page 13) and shortly afterwards two entirely new Triumph cars were announced, the 1800 Series 18T Saloon (shown) and Series 18TR Roadster. Both had a 1776-cc four-cylinder OHV engine. The Saloon featured very attractive 'razor edge' body styling. Production period: March 1946 to January 1949, then continued as 2000 (Renown).

60B: **Triumph** 1800 Roadster, Series 18 TR, was mechanically similar to the 1800 Saloon (except 8 ft 4 in *v.* 9 ft wheelbase), but the 3/5-seat bodywork with its long low lines and curved rear end was in complete contrast. Both cars had a full-width bench-type front seat and steering-column gearchange. Note the triple windscreen wipers. Production period: March 1946 to October 1948.

1946

61A Vauxhall Twelve

61B/C Vauxhall Fourteen

61A: Vauxhall Motors' 1945/46 production programme comprised Ten (Series HIY), Twelve (Series I and HIX) and Fourteen (Series JIB) Saloons. The Twelve was first produced (late 1945 to early 1946) with the 1940-style six-light body (shown), but from March 1946 the same four-light body was used as for the Ten (see next page). The engine was a 1442-cc 35-bhp Four.

61B/C: Vauxhall Fourteen was a six-light saloon with 1781-cc 47·5-bhp six-cylinder engine and a longer wheelbase than the Ten and Twelve (8 ft 9 in v. 8 ft 1¾ in). It was the same as in 1940, but no longer had the chrome radiator grille surround. All models had OHV engines and Dubonnet type IFS.

1946

page 62

62 Vauxhall Fourteen (left) and Twelve (see also 61A)

1946

63A: **Wolseley** Eight could be called a refined edition of the Morris Eight (q.v.). It had an overhead valve version of the 918-cc Morris Eight engine, and with an output of 33 (v. 29·6) bhp was the most powerful (and only OHV) post-war 8 HP car. Naturally it also featured the traditional Wolseley radiator grille, incorporating the illuminated oval badge of the marque. It was produced, only as four-door Saloon, from March 1946 until October 1948.

63B: **Wolseley** Twelve was very similar to its pre-war edition. It was known also as the 12/48 and was in production from December 1945 until October 1948. The engine was a 44-bhp 1548-cc (69·5 × 102 mm) OHV Four. Wheelbase was 8 ft 2 in. Only saloon bodywork was offered, with or without sliding roof.

63C: **Wolseley** Fourteen, or 14/60, was similar to the Twelve but had 6½-in longer wheelbase and 1818-cc (61·5 × 102 mm) six-cylinder OHV engine with two SU carburettors. Also available in 1946 were Ten and Eighteen (18/85) Saloons. These had 1140-cc Four and 2321-cc Six OHV engines respectively.

63B Wolseley Twelve

63A Wolseley Eight

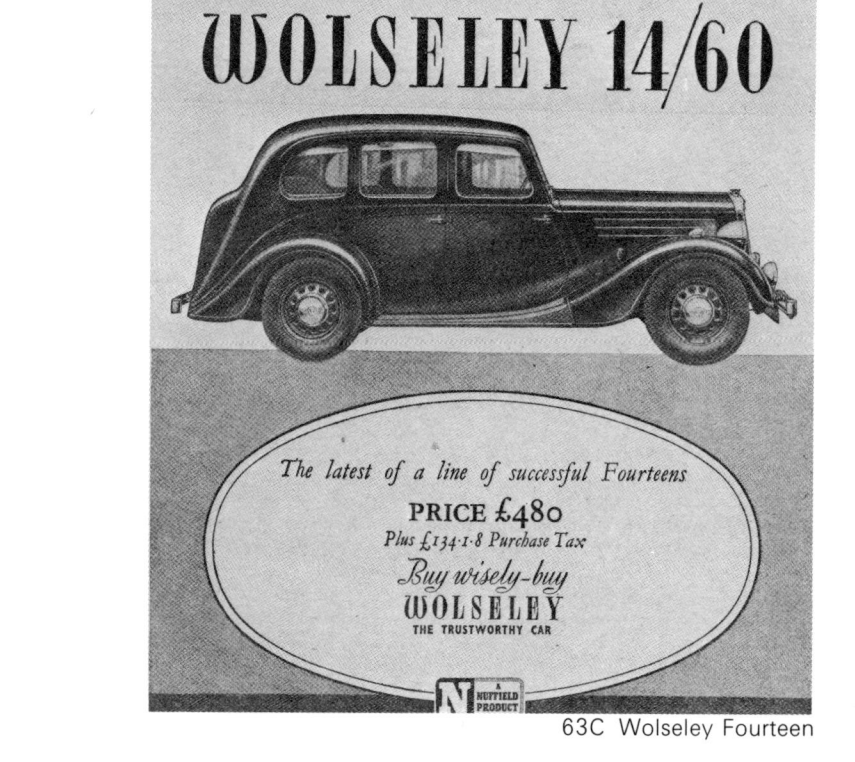

63C Wolseley Fourteen

INDEX

Allard 44
Alvis 4, 44
Armstrong Siddeley 45
Aston Martin 4
Austin 5, 17, 18, 45

Bentley 46
Bristol 47
Buick 42

Daimler 18, 46

Ford 5, 17, 19, 20, 43, 47
Frazer-Nash 47

Hillman 6, 21–23, 48
HRG 48
Humber 7, 17, 23–31, 49–51

Jaguar 34, 52
Jensen 52
Jowett 52

Lagonda 8
Lanchester 53
Lea-Francis 8, 53

MG 54
Morgan 54
Morris 8, 17, 32, 33, 55

Nuffield 33

Riley 9, 55
Rolls-Royce 43, 56
Rover 9, 10, 56

Singer 10, 57
SS 10, 34, 35
Standard 11, 12, 36–41, 57, 58
Sunbeam-Talbot 12, 59

Triumph 13, 14, 60

Vauxhall 15, 61, 62

Willys 33
Wolseley 16, 42, 43, 63

SUMMARY OF MAJOR BRITISH CAR MAKES
1940-1946 (with dates of their existence)

AC	(from 1908)
Alvis	(1920–67)
Armstrong Siddeley	(1919–60)
Austin	(from 1906)
Bentley	(from 1920)
Daimler	(from 1896)
Ford	(from 1911)
Hillman	(from 1907)
Humber	(from 1898)
Jaguar (earlier SS)	(from 1932)
Jowett	(1906–54)
Lagonda	(1906–63)
Lanchester	(1895–1956)
Lea-Francis	(1904–60)*
MG	(from 1924)
Morgan	(from 1910)
Morris	(from 1913)
Riley	(1898–1969)
Rolls-Royce	(from 1904)
Rover	(from 1904)
Singer	(1905–70)
SS (see Jaguar)	
Standard	(1903–63)
Sunbeam-Talbot	(1938–54)
Triumph	(from 1923)
Vauxhall	(from 1903)
Wolseley	(from 1911)

*irregularly

ACKNOWLEDGEMENTS

This book was compiled and written largely from historic source material in the library of the Olyslager Organisation and the Editor's collection, and in addition photographs were kindly provided or loaned by several manufacturers and organisations, notably: Alvis Owner Club (Mr R. A. Cox), Aston Martin Owners Club Ltd (Mr A. A. Archer), British Leyland UK Ltd (Jaguar, Rover and Triumph Divisions), Chrysler UK Ltd, Morgan Motor Company Ltd, Triumph Owners Club (Mr A. C. Cook), and Vauxhall Motors Ltd, as well as a number of private individuals, particularly Messrs John Carter, F. R. Hebron, Glyn Lancaster Jones, Denis Redrupp and B. T. White.

ABBREVIATIONS

bhp   brake horsepower
CR   compression ratio
HP   taxable horsepower (RAC rating)
IFS   independent front suspension
OHC   overhead camshaft (engine)
OHV   overhead valves (engine)
PT   purchase tax
q.v.   *quod vide* (which see)
wb   wheelbase